SHOW DESIGN

daab

Introduction

Trade fairs and showrooms are an increasingly important marketing investment for all kinds of companies and the design of these temporary displays is a growing and constantly changing industry. Both showrooms and trade fair exhibitions serve to showcase and demonstrate a company's new products and services and to convey their brand philosophy. Doing this effectively is not an easy task and best left to marketing and design specialists. Trade fairs are especially tricky as the design of the company's booth is an increasingly powerful sales strategy. The importance of these professional shows is clearly reflected in the huge number and variety of these events held all over the world. With thousands of visitors seeing yours and thousand of other companies's booths, the pressure is on to make yours stand out from the rest. Considering the visitor will spend no more than a maximum of 15 minutes at each stand, designers need to clearly get the company's message across in the least possible time, using innovative solutions and technologies. Similarly, showrooms are a way of advertising the product, making the layout and positioning of the wares a carefully considered task. The word 'showroom' may evoke images of the first purpose-built car showrooms, which began to proliferate at the time of the mass-production of cars at the beginning of the 20th century. Nowadays, however, a huge array of products, from sanitary ware and electronics to upholstery, fashion, lighting and furniture, to mention but a few, are investing in showrooms of all sizes and fashions. This book intends to show the great lengths some companies will go to in order to be seen and, more importantly, to be remembered. The following pages will present a wide selection of trade fairs and showrooms from around the world created by established and emerging designers.

Handelsmessen und Showrooms gewinnen als Marketingmaßnahme für alle Arten von Unternehmen immer mehr an Bedeutung. Das Design dieser zeitlich befristeten Ausstellungen ist eine wachsende und sich ständig wandelnde Branche. Sowohl in Showrooms als auch auf Handelsmessen haben Unternehmen die Möglichkeit, ihre neuen Produkte und Dienstleistungen zu präsentieren und die Firmenphilosophie vorzustellen. Dies effektiv durchzuführen ist keine leichte Aufgabe, die am besten Marketing- und Designspezialisten überlassen werden sollte. Handelsmessen sind besonders schwierig, da das Design des Stands eines Unternehmens eine zunehmend wichtige Verkaufsstrategie darstellt. Die Bedeutung dieser Fachmessen ist deutlich ersichtlich an der großen Zahl und Vielfalt, mit der sie auf der ganzen Welt stattfinden. Da Tausende von Besuchern sowohl Ihren als auch den Messestand Tausender anderer Unternehmen sehen, ist der Druck groß, einen Stand zu entwerfen, der sich vom Rest abhebt. Wenn man bedenkt, dass ein Besucher nicht mehr als höchstens 15 Minuten an jedem Stand verbringt, müssen Designer in kürzester Zeit und mit Hilfe von innovativen Lösungen und Techniken die Botschaft des Unternehmens übermitteln. Auch Showrooms sind eine Art der Produktwerbung, weswegen die Anordnung und Platzierung der Waren wohl bedacht sein sollte. Das Wort „Showroom" ruft möglicherweise Bilder der ersten Autoshowrooms hervor, die sich zu Beginn der Massenproduktion von Kraftfahrzeugen Anfang des 20. Jahrhunderts verbreiteten. Heutzutage jedoch gibt es Showrooms in allen Größen und Arten für eine breite Palette von Produkten, von Sanitärkeramik und Elektronik bis zu Mode, Beleuchtung und Möbeln, um nur einige Beispiele zu nennen. Dieses Buch möchte zeigen, dass einige Unternehmen keine Mühe scheuen, um gesehen zu werden und – wichtiger noch – zu erreichen, dass man sich an sie erinnert. Auf den folgenden Seiten wird eine Vielfalt von Handelsmessen und Showrooms vorgestellt, die sowohl von bekannten als auch von neuen Designern entworfen wurden.

Las ferias de muestras y los *showrooms* son una inversión de *marketing* cada vez más importante para compañías de todo tipo, y el diseño de estas exposiciones temporales representa una industria creciente y en constante cambio. Tanto los *showrooms* como las ferias de muestras sirven para exhibir y presentar los nuevos productos y servicios de una compañía y para comunicar la filosofía de su marca. Hacer esto de manera efectiva no resulta tarea sencilla, de modo que conviene dejar el trabajo en manos de especialistas de *marketing* y diseño. Las ferias de muestras son particularmente complejas, puesto que el diseño del *stand* de la compañía se ha convertido en una estrategia de ventas cada vez más poderosa. La importancia de las ferias profesionales se refleja en la variedad de eventos de esta clase que se multiplican alrededor del mundo. Cuando innumerables visitantes miran miles de *stands* de otras tantas compañías, hay una enorme presión para hacer que el propio destaque entre los demás. Considerando el hecho de que el visitante pasará como máximo 15 minutos en cada *stand*, los diseñadores tienen que transmitir claramente el mensaje de la compañía en el menor tiempo posible, utilizando para ello soluciones y tecnologías innovadoras. Asimismo, los *showrooms* son una forma de hacer publicidad del producto, por lo cual la disposición y distribución de los objetos supone una labor en la que se debe tener mucho cuidado. La palabra *showroom* puede evocar imágenes de los primeros *showrooms* construidos a medida para exhibir coches, que comenzaron a proliferar en la época de producción masiva de automóviles, a comienzos del siglo XX. Sin embargo, hoy en día una gran variedad de empresas que producen desde utensilios sanitarios o electrónicos hasta tapicería, moda, iluminación y muebles, por mencionar tan sólo unos cuantos sectores de producción, están invirtiendo en *showrooms* de todos los tamaños y modelos. Este libro pretende mostrar el esfuerzo que algunas compañías hacen para ser vistas y, lo que es más importante aún, para ser recordadas. Las siguientes páginas presentan una amplia selección de ferias de muestras y de *showrooms* de todo el mundo, creadas por diseñadores reconocidos y noveles.

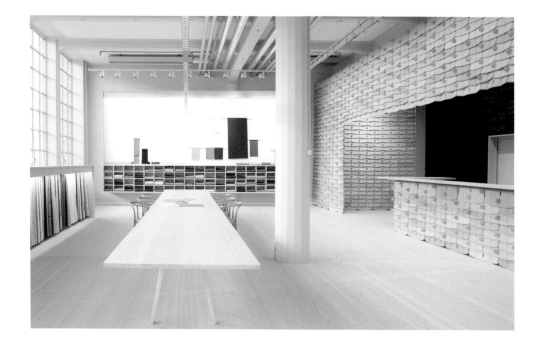

Les salons professionnels et show-rooms représentent, tous types de société confondus, un investissement marketing toujours plus important. Le design de ces expositions temporaires constitue une industrie montante, en constante évolution. Les show-rooms et salons professionnels ont le même objectif : exposer et présenter les nouveaux produits et services des compagnies tout en transmettant la philosophie de leur enseigne. Pour un design efficace de ces salons, tâche qui n'est pas des plus faciles, il vaut donc mieux faire appel à des spécialistes du marketing et du design. En effet, les salons professionnels sont particulièrement complexes à réaliser, le design des stands des compagnies devenant un élément de stratégie de vente de plus en plus puissant. L'importance de ces évènements professionnels se reflète clairement dans le nombre considérable et la variété de ces manifestations de par le monde. Face aux milliers de visiteurs regardant ton stand en même temps que des milliers d'autres de sociétés concurrentes, une énorme pression s'exerce pour que le tien se démarque du reste. Le visiteur ne passant que 15 minutes au maximum devant chaque stand, les designers doivent transmettre, clairement et le plus vite possible, le message de la compagnie, par le biais de solutions et technologies innovantes. De même, les show-rooms sont une manière de faire de la publicité pour le produit. Ce mot anglais n'est d'ailleurs pas sans évoquer les images des tout premiers show-rooms spécialement destinés aux voitures, qui se sont multipliés lors de la fabrication automobile en série, au début du XXe siècle. Cependant, de nos jours, cette image a évolué : en effet, un immense éventail de sociétés offrant leurs produits allant d'articles sanitaires au capitonnage, de la mode à l'éclairage et de l'électronique au mobilier, pour ne citer que ceux-là, investissent dans les show-rooms de tailles et styles divers. Cet ouvrage essaie de présenter la panoplie de moyens que certaines sociétés sont prêtes à déployer pour être vues, et qui plus est, être remarquées. Et, au fil de ces pages, vous découvrirez une large sélection de salons professionnels et de show-rooms du monde entier créés par des designers confirmés ou émergents.

Le fiere commerciali e gli *showroom* costituiscono un investimento in marketing sempre più rilevante per imprese d'ogni tipo, e il design di queste esposizioni provvisorie rappresenta un settore in crescita e in costante cambiamento. Sia gli *showroom* sia le fiere commerciali sono mezzi con cui le imprese esibiscono e presentano i loro nuovi prodotti e servizi, oltre a trasmettere la propria filosofia di marca. Riuscirci è un compito tutt'altro che facile, che è meglio riservare a specialisti del marketing e del design. Le fiere commerciali sono particolarmente insidiose dato che il design dello stand dell'impresa è una strategia commerciale di sempre maggior impatto. L'importanza di questi saloni professionali si rispecchia chiaramente nell'immensa quantità e varietà di eventi di questo genere celebrati in tutto il mondo. Quando innumerevoli visitatori guardano il tuo stand tra quello di migliaia di altre imprese, è forte la pressione per far sì che il proprio spicchi sul resto. Considerando che il visitatore passerà un massimo di soli 15 minuti in ogni stand, i designer devono trasmettere il messaggio dell'impresa in modo chiaro nel più breve tempo possibile, utilizzando a questo scopo soluzioni e tecnologie innovative. Analogamente, gli *showroom* costituiscono un mezzo di promozione del prodotto, per cui la distribuzione e la disposizione della merce diventano aspetti da considerare con attenzione. La parola «showroom» potrebbe evocare l'immagine dei primi *showroom* creati per le auto, che cominciarono a proliferare all'epoca della produzione di massa di autovetture all'inizio del XX secolo. Oggi, tuttavia, un gran numero di imprese produttrici di articoli che vanno dai sanitari all'elettronica, passando per la tappezzeria, la moda, l'illuminazione e l'arredamento, per citarne solo alcuni, stanno investendo nella creazione di *showroom* di tutti i tipi e dimensioni. Questo libro vuole mostrare fino a che punto sono disposte ad arrivare alcune imprese per essere viste e, soprattutto, ricordate. Le pagine che seguono presentano una vasta selezione di fiere commerciali e *showroom* di tutto il mondo creati da designer affermati ed emergenti.

A. ML UND PARTNER/PROF. MATTHIAS LOEBERMANN | NUREMBERG
STAND FOR EUROPET AT INTERZOO
Nuremberg, Germany | 2004

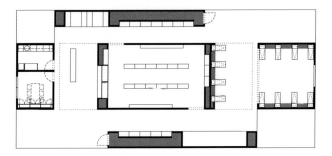

ÁNGEL GORDON | BARCELONA
PORTAE SHOWROOM
Barcelona, Spain | 2004

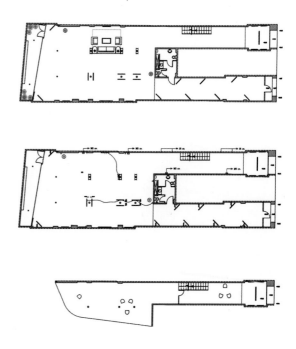

BARBOSA SPACE PROJECTS | GRADO
STAND FOR ABDÓN & LUCAS AT INTERNATIONAL FURNITURE FAIR VALENCIA (FIM)
Valencia, Spain | 2005

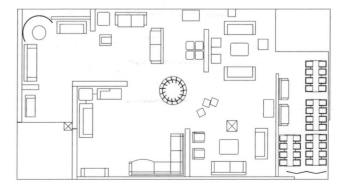

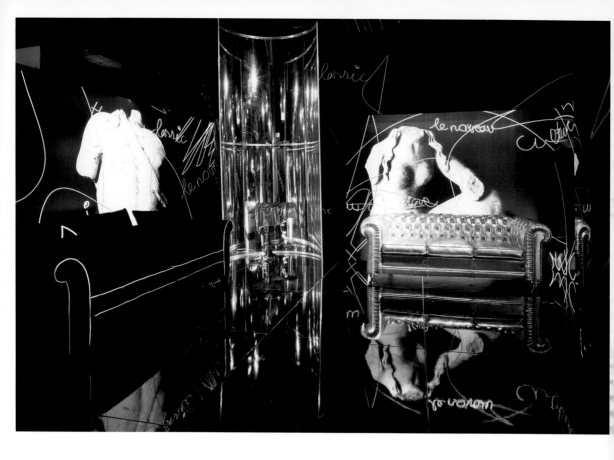

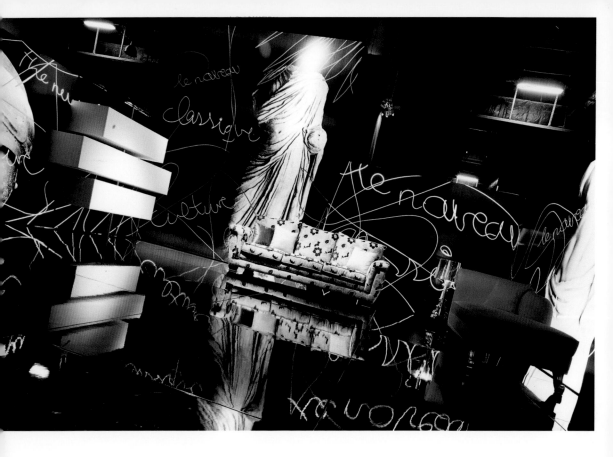

BISAZZA DESIGN STUDIO/CARLO DAL BIANCO | ALTE DI MONTECCHIO MAGGIORE
BISAZZA SHOWROOM
Barcelona, Spain | 2006

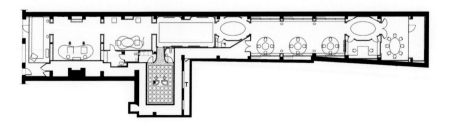

BRUCE GOODSIR | MELBOURNE
E.G.ETAL SHOWROOM
Melbourne, Australia | 2004

BURATTI & BATTISTON ARCHITECTS | MILAN
STAND FOR ACERBIS INTERNATIONAL AT SALONE DEL MOBILE
Milan, Italy | 2006

C. M. INTERIORS, ESIETE/JAVIER PEREDA | BARCELONA
MEGA SPORT S.A. SHOWROOMS
Barcelona, Spain | 2006

CADOSCH & ZIMMERMANN | ZURICH
STAND FOR ETERNIT AG AND SWISSPOR AG AT SWISSBAU
Basel, Switzerland | 2005

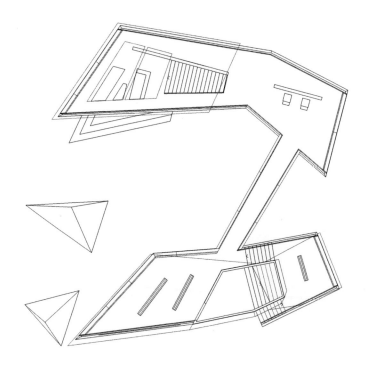

CHELSEA ATELIER ARCHITECT | NEW YORK
REEM ACRA SHOWROOM
New York, USA | 2003

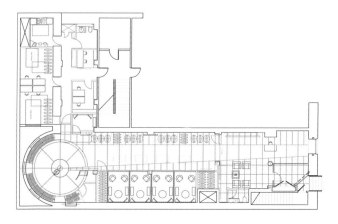

lt, ich wär ein Teppich.

Cos

Cos

Tec Line

CHRISTIAN WERNER | HOLLENSTEDT/APPEL
STAND FOR CARPET CONCEPT AT ORGATEC
Cologne, Germany | 2006

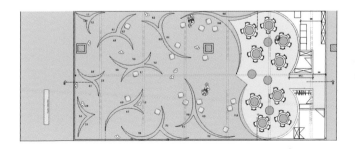

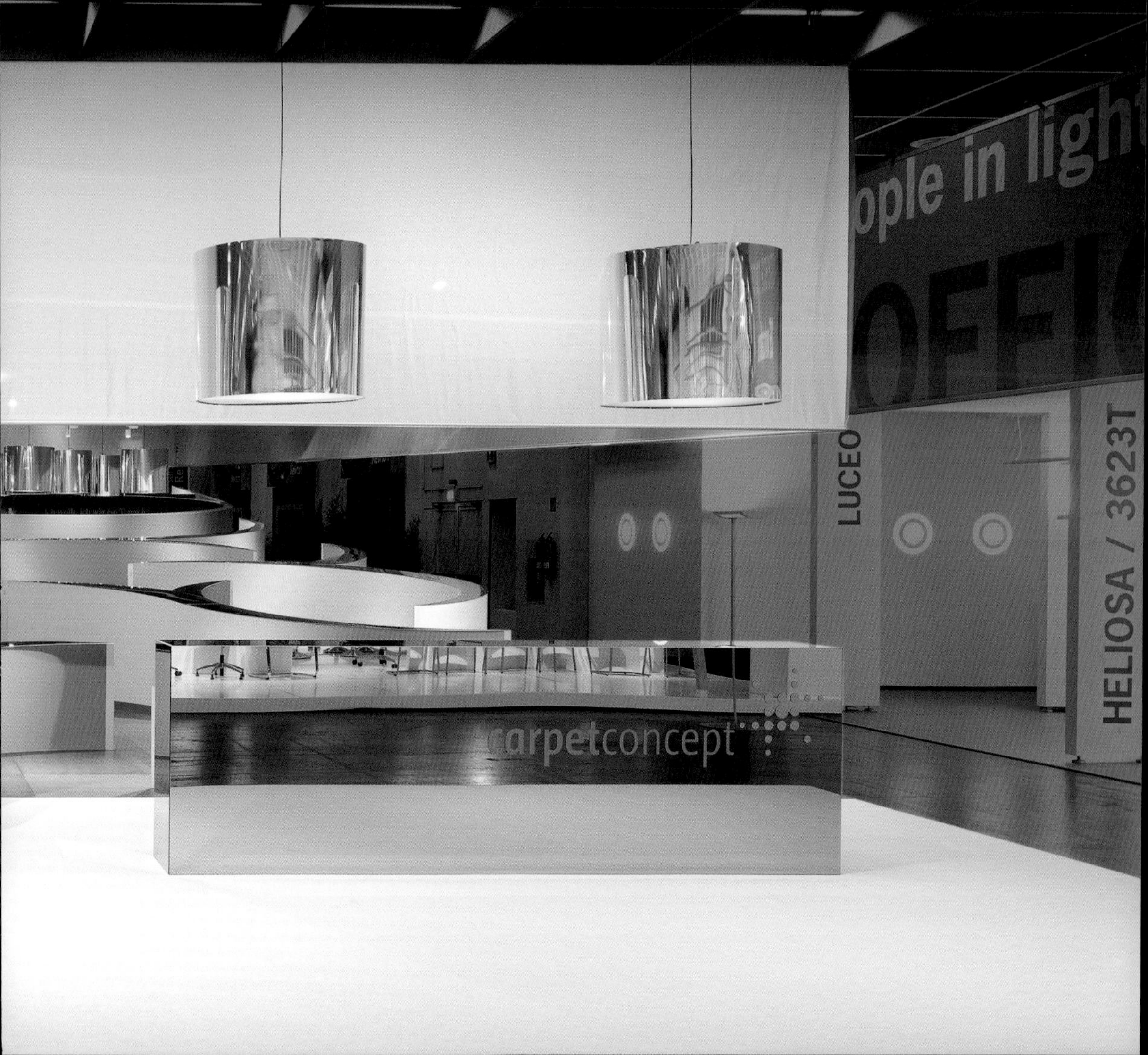
ople in ligh
OFFIC
LUCEO
HELIOSA / 3623T
carpetconcept

Ich wollt, ich wär ein Teppich.
Dann könnt ich jeden Morgen liegen bleibe[n]

[i]st die Arbeit weniger langweilig als das Ver[gnügen]

CHRISTIAN WERNER | HOLLENSTEDT/APPEL
STAND FOR ROLF BENZ AT THE INTERNATIONAL FURNISHING SHOW (IMM)
Cologne, Germany | 2006

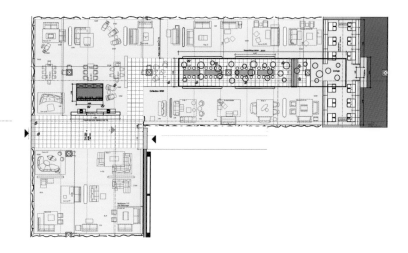

CJ STUDIO | TAIPEI

SHOWROOM FOR STEPHANE DOU & CHANGLEE YUGIN

Taichung, Taiwan | 2005

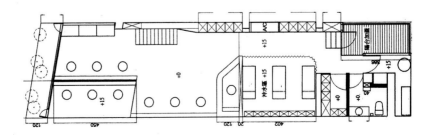

STEPHANEDOUCHANGLEEYUGIN

CLAUDIO CARMONA PARCERISA | BARCELONA
ROSA CLARÀ SHOWROOM
Barcelona, Spain | 2005

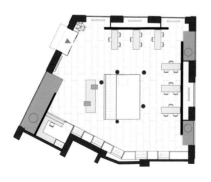 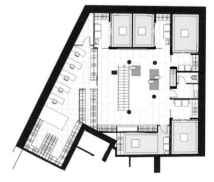

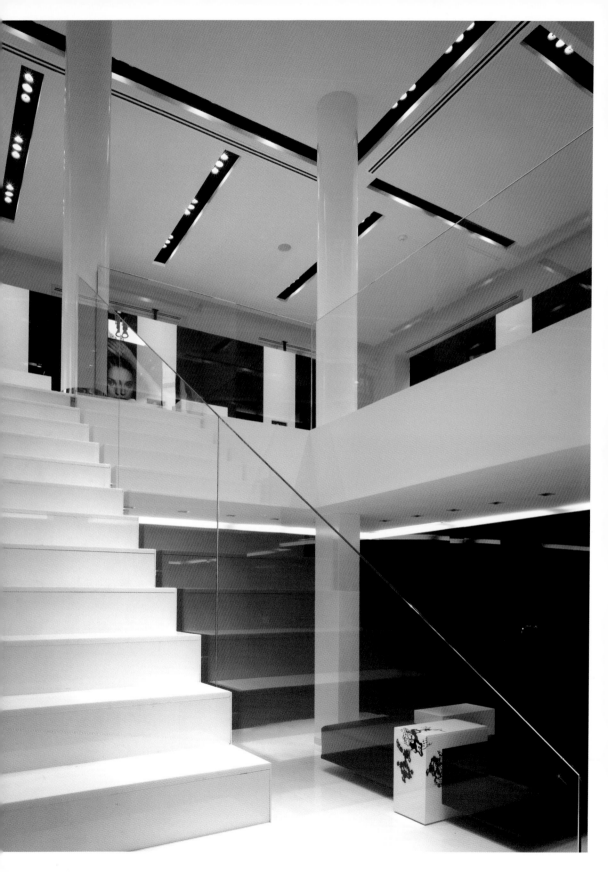

"Se fossi la regina del paese della cuccagna, per me
esisterebbero solo crêpes con la marmellata!"

Lisa, 4 anni

here would
lade pancakes to eat!"

Lisa, 4 years old

"I I were Queen of Lu
onl

D'ART DESIGN GRUPPE | NEUSS
STAND FOR ALNO AG AT EUROCUCINA
Milan, Italy | 2006

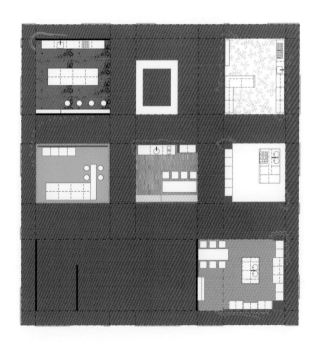

D'ART DESIGN GRUPPE | NEUSS
STAND FOR D'ART DESIGN GRUPPE AT EUROSHOP
Düsseldorf, Germany | 2005

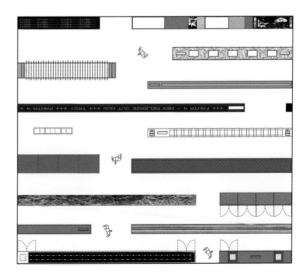

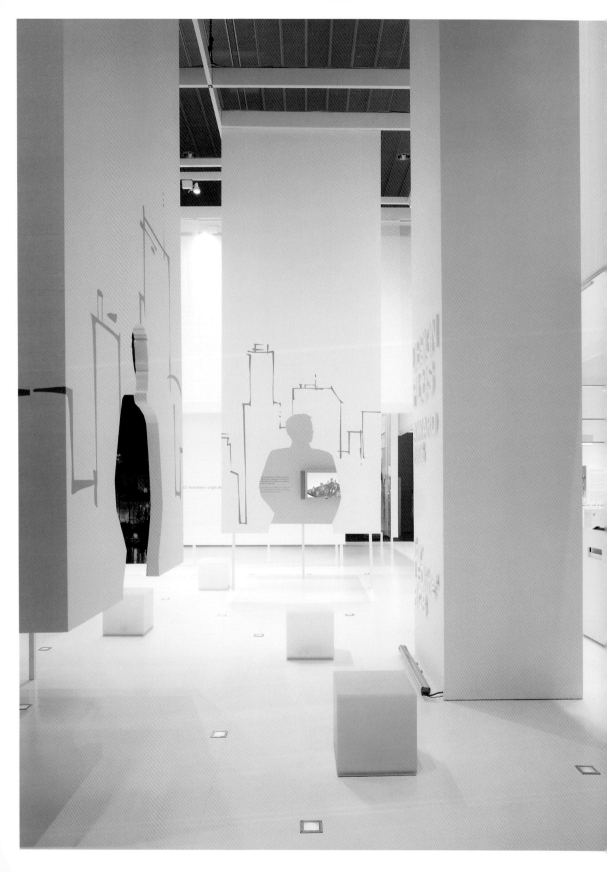

D'ART DESIGN GRUPPE | NEUSS
STAND FOR PHILIPS LIGHTING AT LIGHT & BUILDING
Frankfurt, Germany | 2006

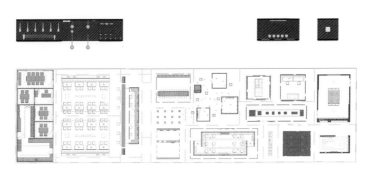

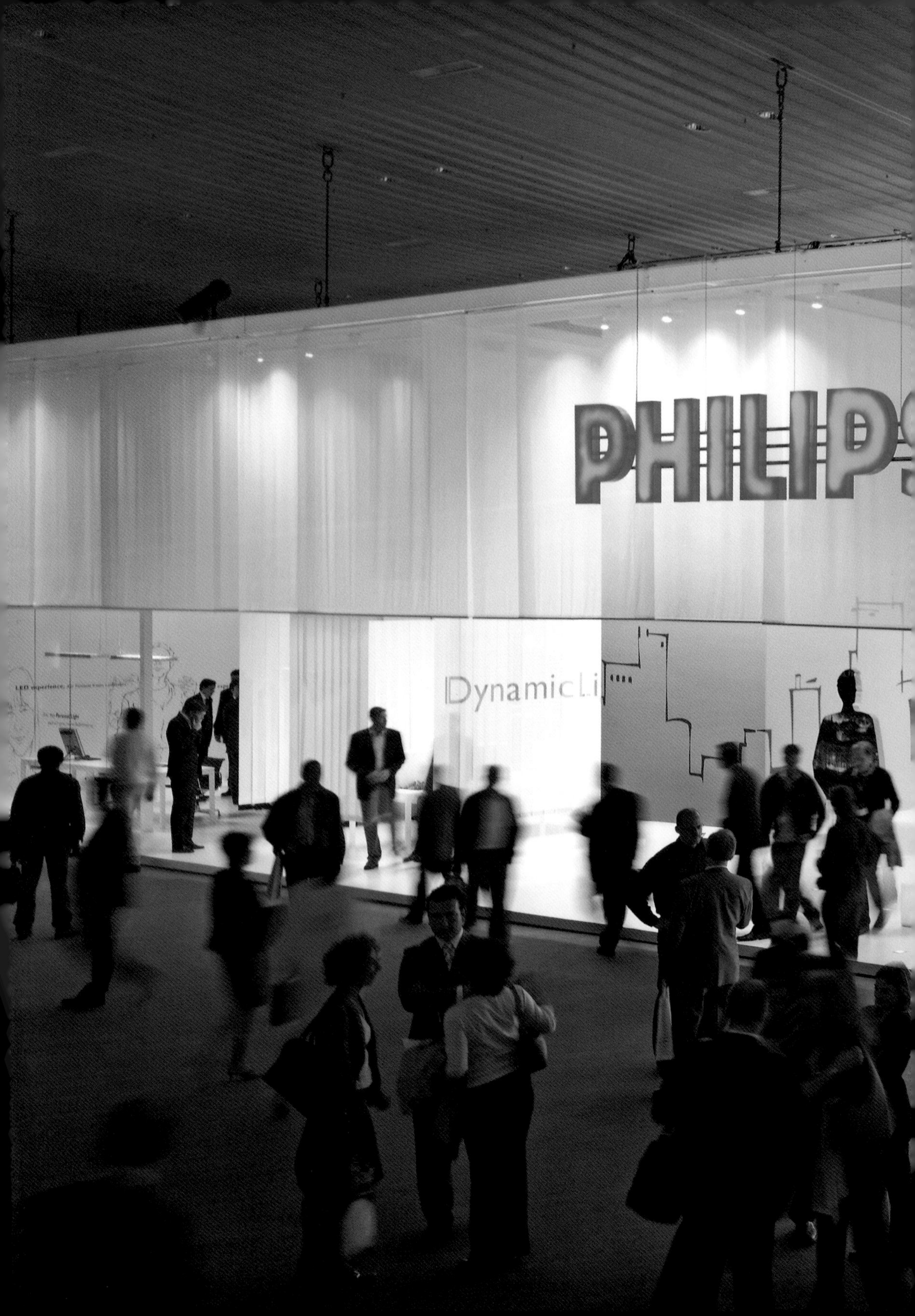
PHILIPS
DynamicLi

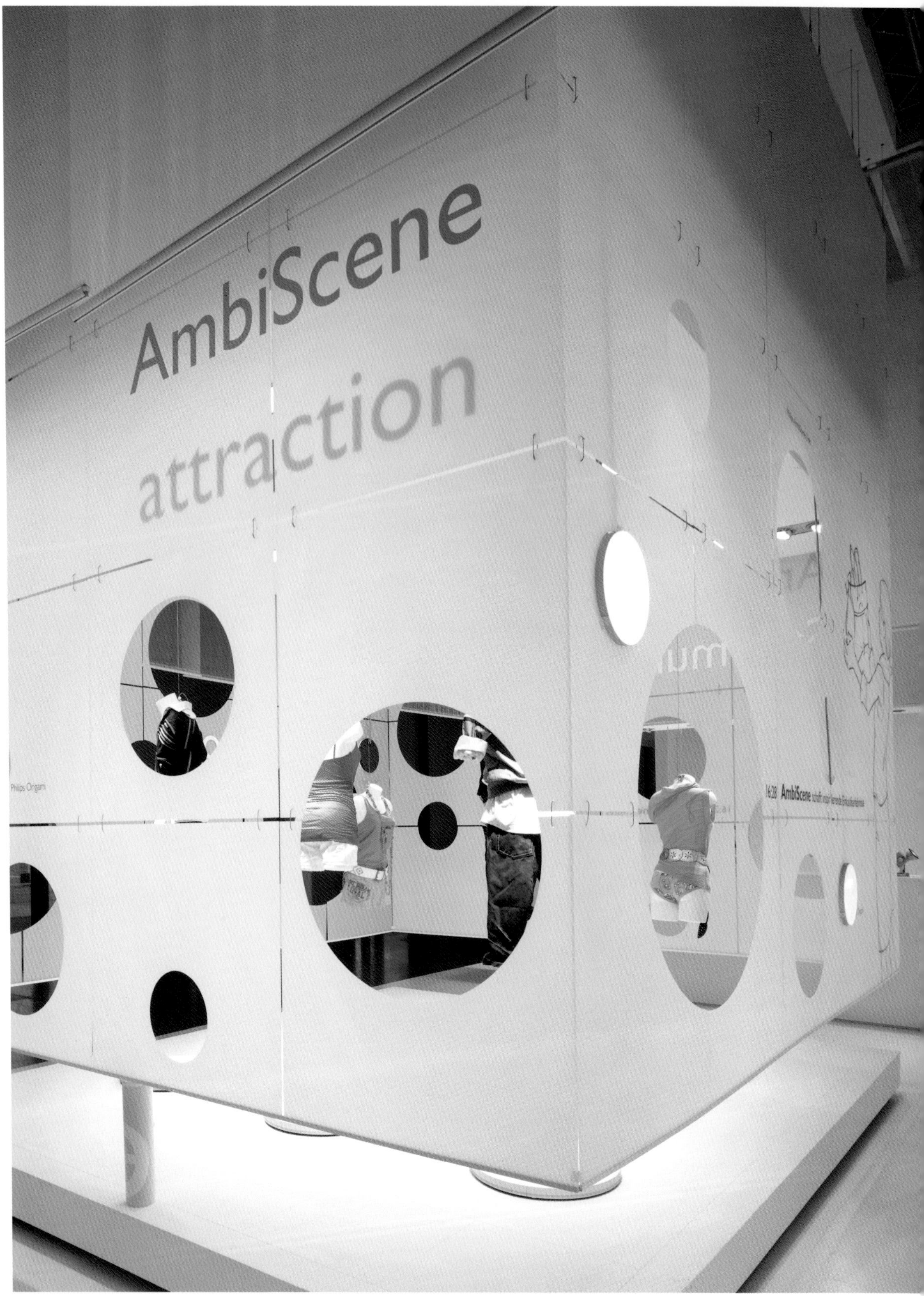
AmbiScene
attraction
Philips Origami
16:28 AmbiScene

DESIGNRICHTUNG/JÉRÔME GESSAGA & CHRISTOF HINDERMANN | ZURICH
DENZ AG OFFICE ARCHITECTURE SHOWROOM
Bern, Switzerland | 2005

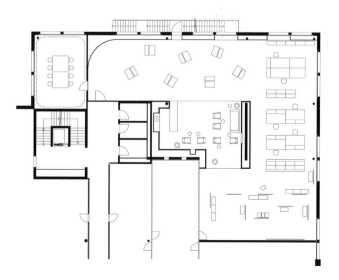

DESIGNRICHTUNG/JÉRÔME GESSAGA & CHRISTOF HINDERMANN | ZURICH
GEBERIT VERTRIEBS AG SHOWROOM
Jona, Switzerland | 2003

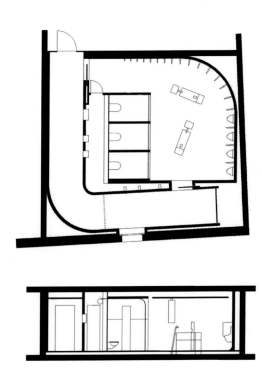

DOMINIC NIELS HAAG | ZURICH
STAND FOR SIA AT SWISSBAU
Basel, Switzerland | 2005

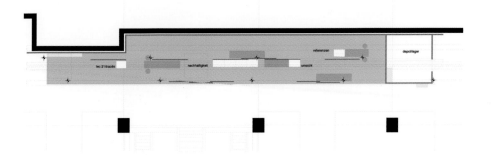

Nachhaltiges Bauen – Hochbau

schaft
Gebäudesubstanz
Anlagekosten
Betrieb- und Unterhaltskosten

Umwelt
    Baustoffe
    Betriebsenergie
    Boden / Landschaft
    Infrastruktur

Construction durable – Bâtiment

SIA 112/1

Société
Vie en commun
Aménagement
Exploitation/Viabilité
Confort/Santé

Économie
Substance du bâtiment
Frais d'investissement
Frais d'exploitation et d'entretien

Environnement
Matériaux de construction
Énergie d'exploitation
Sol/Paysage
Infrastructure

DUAL OFFICE | SAN FRANCISCO
ECHO HANDBAG SHOWROOM
New York, USA | 2004

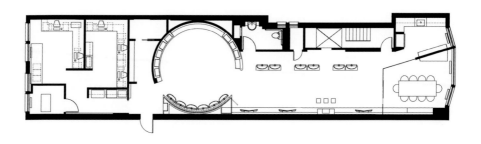

ESTUDI AROLA | BARCELONA
STAND FOR SANTA & COLE AT LIGHT & BUILDING
Frankfurt, Germany | 2006

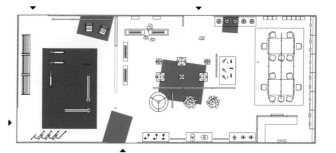

FRANCESC RIFÉ | BARCELONA
PARKHOUSE STUDIO SHOWROOM
Barcelona, Spain | 2005

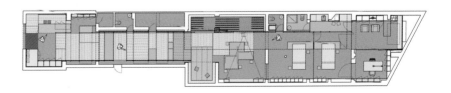

FRANCESC RIFÉ | BARCELONA
STAND FOR BORDONABE AT OFITEC
Madrid, Spain | 2006

FRANCESC RIFÉ | BARCELONA
STAND FOR MARTÍNEZ OTERO AT INTERNATIONAL FURNITURE FAIR VALENCIA (FIM)
Valencia, Spain | 2006

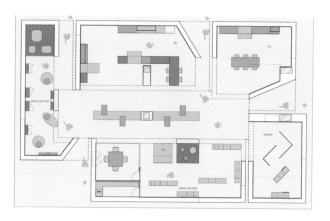

GIORGIO BORRUSO DESIGN | MARINA DEL REY
SNAIDERO USA SHOWROOM
Los Angeles, USA | 2005

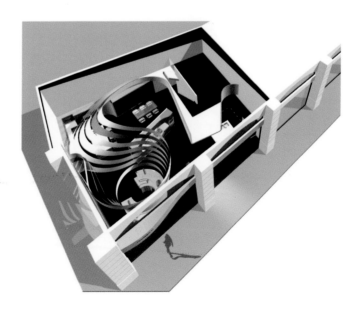

IGNASI BONJOCH | BARCELONA
STAND FOR BIOSCA & BOTEY AT CONSTRUMAT
Barcelona, Spain | 2005

JACI FOTI-LOWE | MELBOURNE
HUB FURNITURE LIVING LIGHTING SHOWROOM
Melbourne, Australia | 2006

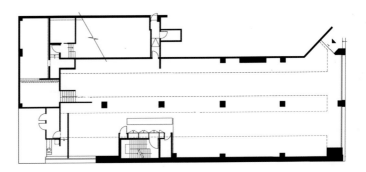

JOAN ANGUITA & RAFAEL BERENGENA ARQUITECTOS | BARCELONA
CASA DELFÍN S.A. SHOWROOM
Tárrega, Spain | 2006

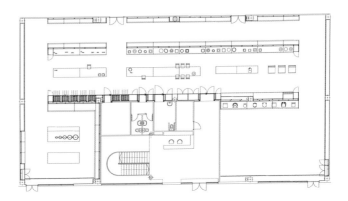

JOAN LAO | BARCELONA
JOAN LAO SHOWROOM
Barcelona, Spain | 2005

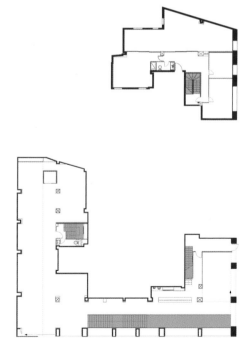

JUMP STUDIOS | LONDON
STAND FOR LEVI'S AT BREAD & BUTTER BARCELONA
Barcelona, Spain | 2006

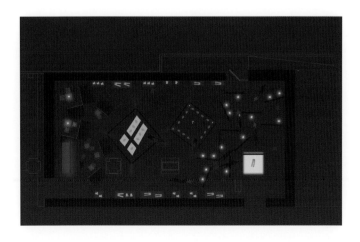

JÜRGEN MAYER H., ALESSANDRA RAPONI | BERLIN
STAND FOR NYA NORDISKA AT DESIGN ANNUAL
Frankfurt, Germany | 2006

KNOLL/KAREN STONE | NEW YORK
KNOLL SHOWROOM
Santa Monica, USA | 2005

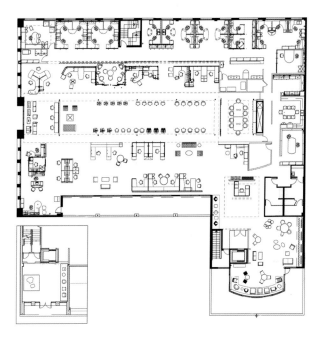

KUHLMANN LEAVITT | ST. LOUIS
STAND FOR FORMICA CORPORATION AT INTERNATIONAL HOME BUILDERS' SHOW (IBS)
Orlando, USA | 2006

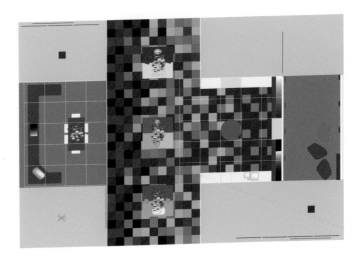

LANDINI ASSOCIATES | SURRY HILLS
HARROLDS SHOWROOM
Melbourne, Australia | 2005

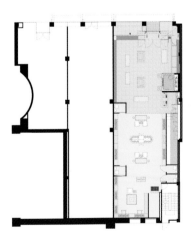 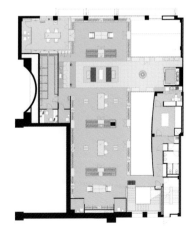

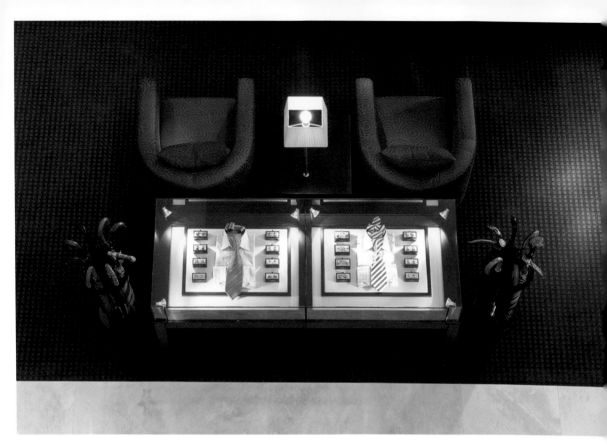

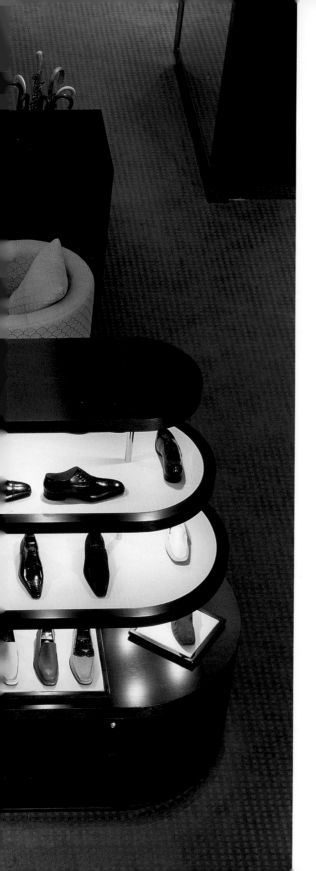

LOC ARQUITECTOS/CASILLAS & SÁNCHEZ MERCHÁN | MADRID
STAND FOR ICEX AT EXPORTA
Valencia, Spain | 2003

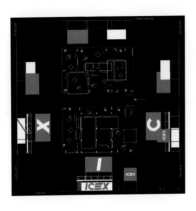
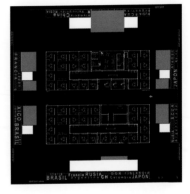

APRENDIENDO
A EXPORTAR

EXPERIÈNCIES EXPORTADORES

CASOS DE ÉXITO   7"

EXPORTAR,
TAN FÁCIL COMO NECESARIO   21"

PAOLO CESARETTI, LAURA DANIELI | MILAN
HATRIA/GRUPPO MARAZZI SHOWROOM
Modena, Italy | 2004

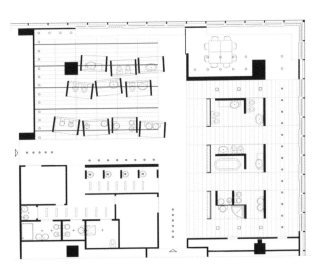

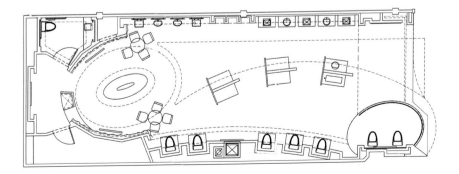

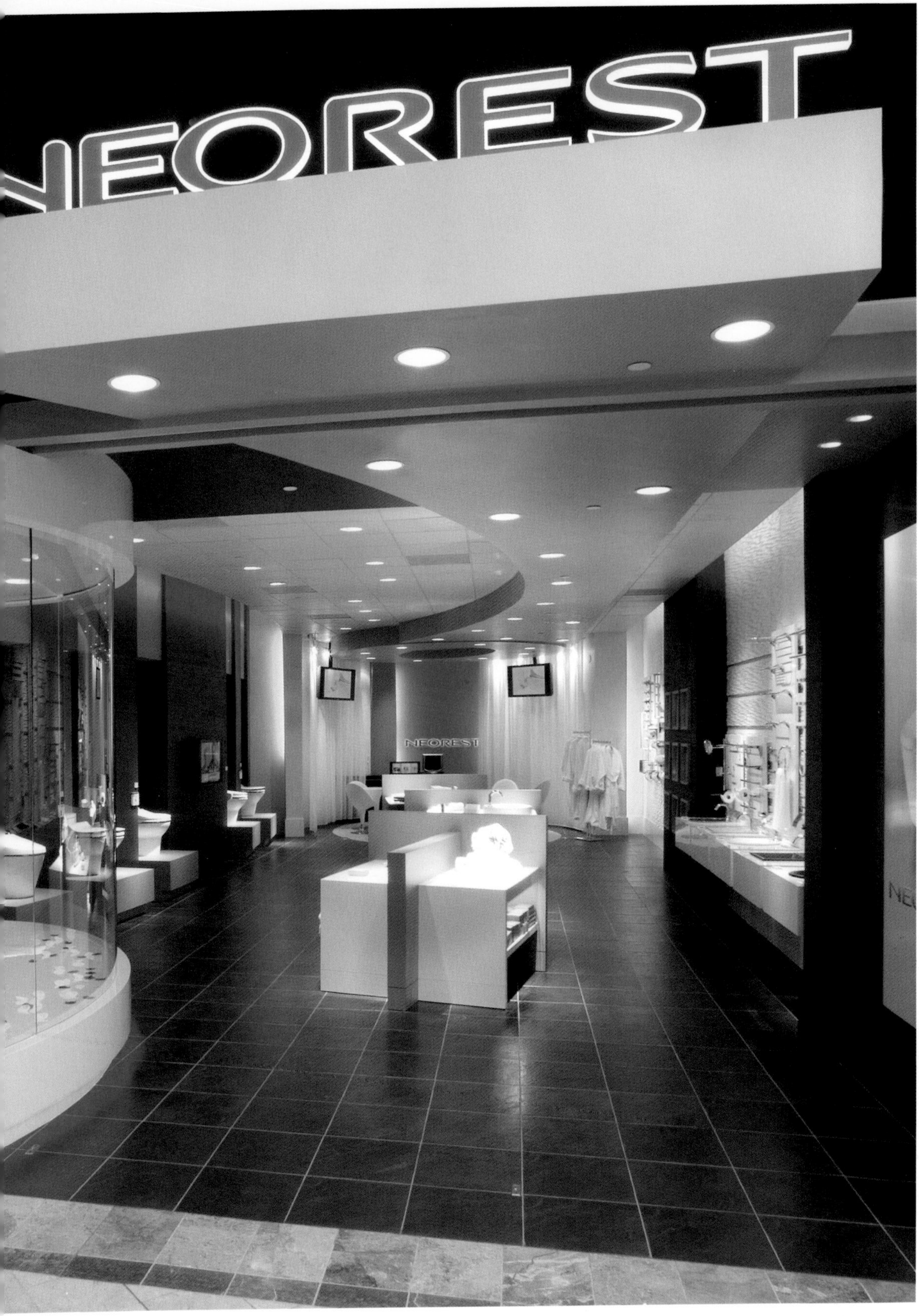
NEOREST
NEOREST

PS+A/LUDOVICA & ROBERTO PALOMBA | MILAN
ZUCCHETTI SHOWROOM
Fundació Foto Colectània, Barcelona, Spain | 2005

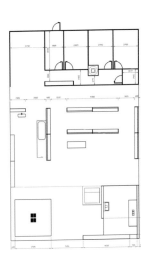 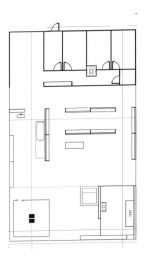

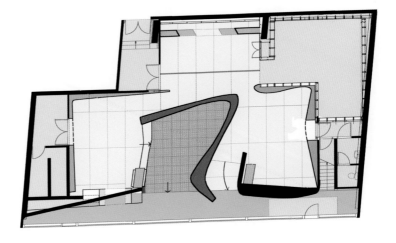

RONAN & ERWAN BOUROULLEC | PARIS
KVADRAT SHOWROOM
Stockholm, Sweden | 2006

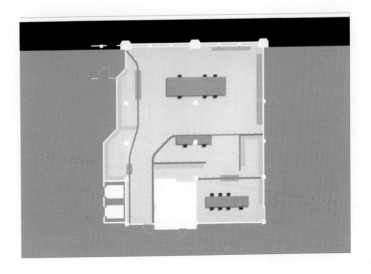

SAETA ESTUDI/BET CANTALLOPS, PERE ORTEGA | BARCELONA
STAND FOR LAYETANA AT BARCELONA MEETING POINT
Barcelona, Spain | 2006

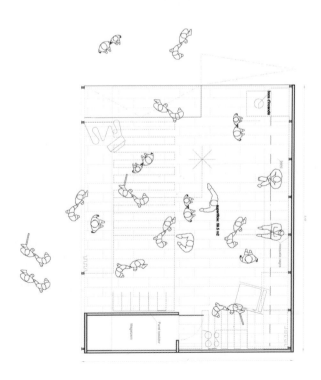

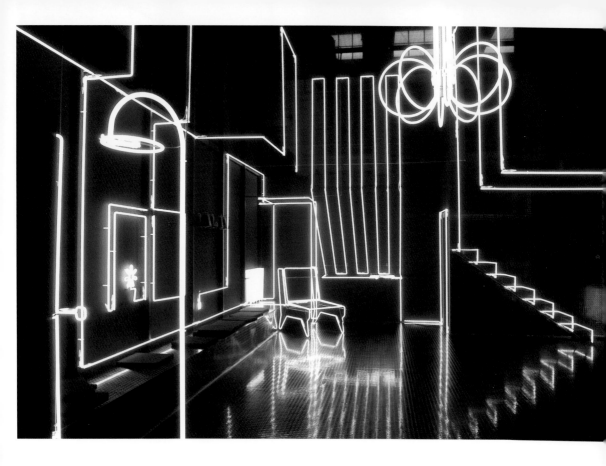

SCHINDLERARCHITEKTEN | STUTTGART
STAND FOR ARMSTRONG DLW AG AT DOMOTEX
Hannover, Germany | 2006

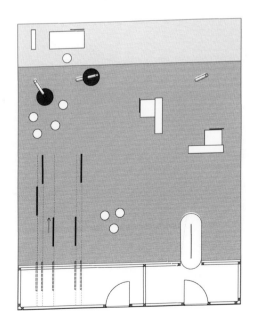

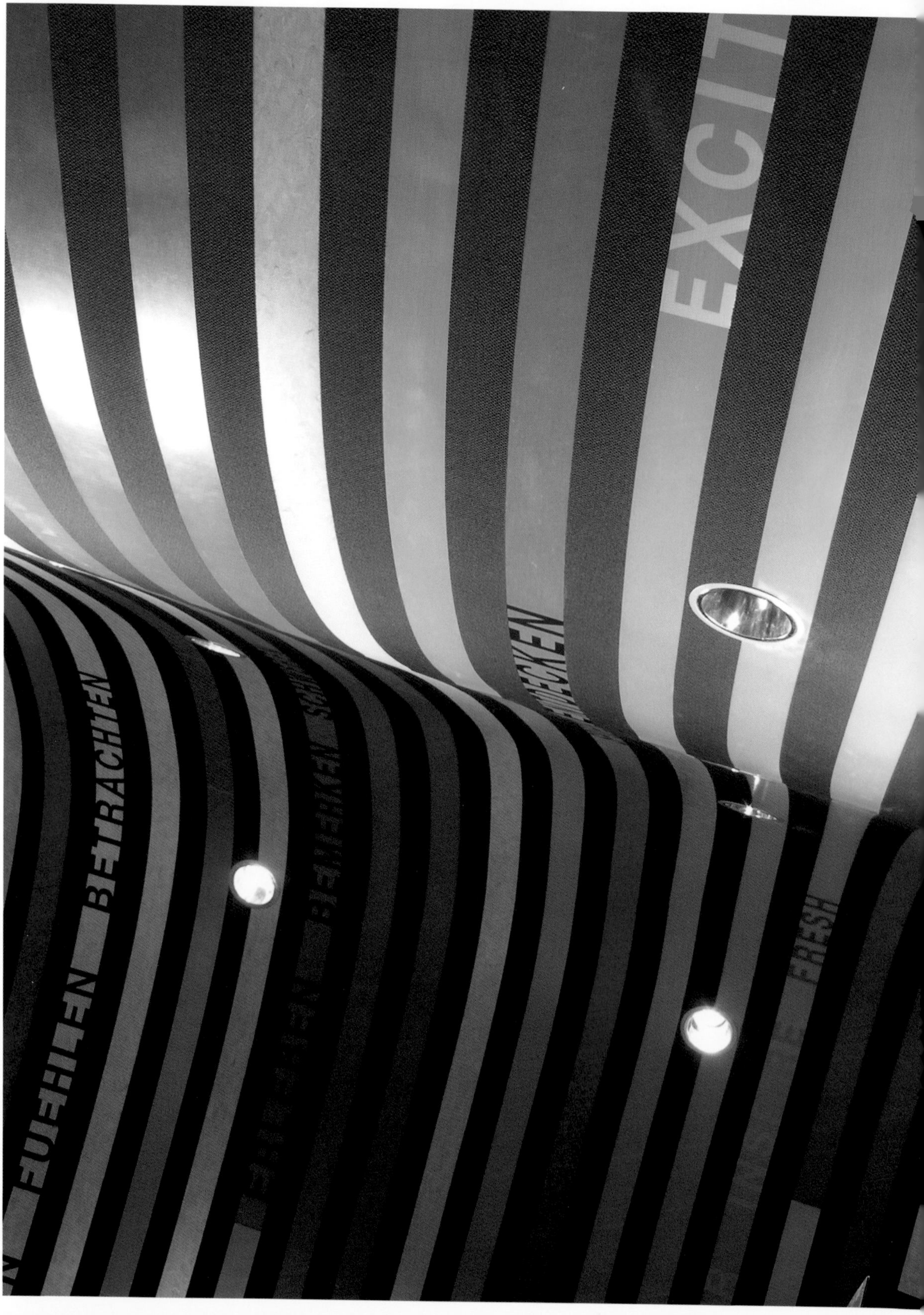
EXCIT
BETRACHTEN
FUEHLEN
FRESH

SCHMIDHUBER & KAINDL | MUNICH
SAMSUNG BRAND SHOP
Seoul, Korea | 2005

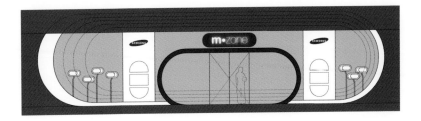

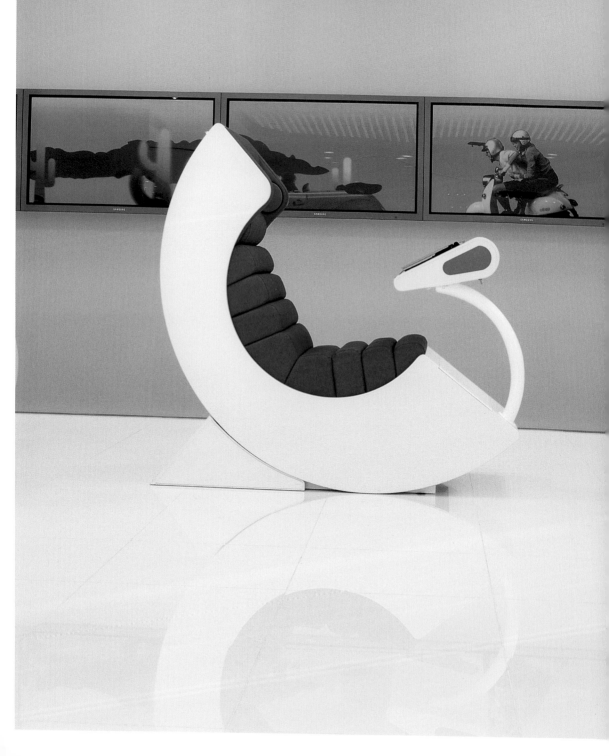

SCHMIDHUBER & PARTNER, KMS TEAM | MUNICH
STAND FOR O2 AT CEBIT
Berlin, Germany | 2006

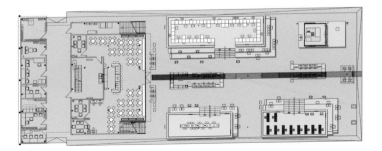

STUDIOMARTINO.5 | ROME
CROVATO SHOWROOM
Milan, Italy | 2005

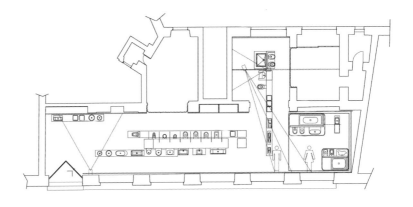

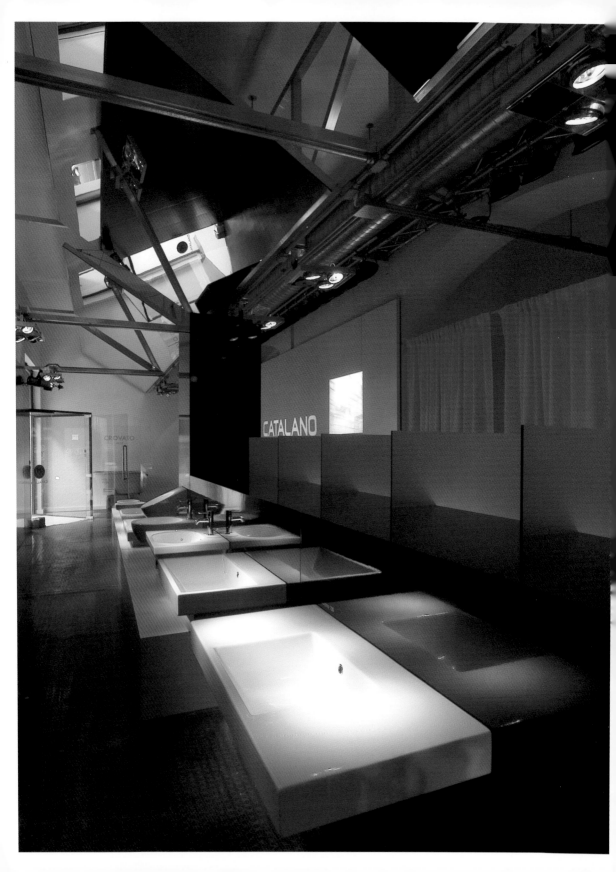

TOTEMS COMMUNICATION & ARCHITECTURE | STUTTGART
STAND FOR BERTRANDT AT INTERNATIONAL MOTOR SHOW (IAA)
Frankfurt, Germany | 2005

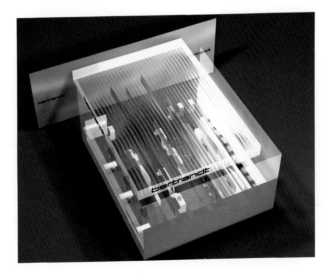

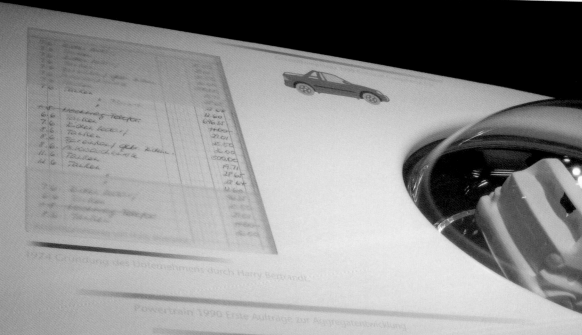

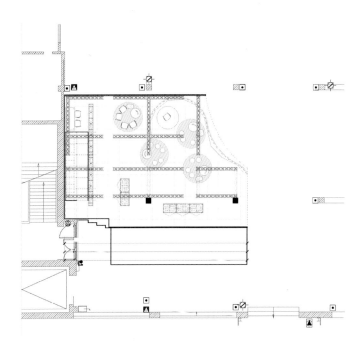

A. ML und Partner/Prof. Matthias Loebermann
Praterstrasse 30, 90429 Nuremburg, Germany
P +49 911 510 9031
F +49 911 510 9032
mail@aml-partner.de
www.aml-partner.de
Stand for Europet at Interzoo
Photos: © Mila Hacke

Ángel Gordon
C/Enric Granados 8 pral. 2ª, 08007 Barcelona, Spain
P +34 686 956 910
F +34 686 956 910
Portae Showroom
Photos: © Gogortza & Llorella

Barbosa Space Projects
Av. Vistalegre 43, 33820 Grado, Spain
P +34 985 272 292
F +34 985 272 292
info@barbosasp.com
www.barbosasp.com
Stand for Abdón & Lucas at International
Furniture Fair Valencia (FIM)
Photos: © Luis Hevia

Bisazza Design Studio/Carlo Dal Bianco
Bisazza Spa, Viale Milano 56, 36075 Alte di Montecchio
Maggiore (VI), Italy
P +39 444 707 511
F +39 444 492 088
studio@carlodalbianco.it
www.bisazza.com
Bisazza Showroom
Photos: © Andrea Resmini

Bruce Goodsir
167 Flinders Lane, 3000 Melbourne, Australia
P +61 396 395 111
F +61 396 395 111
emma@egetal.com.au
www.egetal.com.au
E.g.etal Showroom
Photos: © Trevor Mein

Buratti & Battiston Architects
Via Cellini 5, 20020 Busto Garolfo, Milan, Italy
P +39 331 569 575
F +39 331 569 063
studio@burattibattiston.it
www.burattibattiston.it
Stand for Acerbis International at Salone del Mobile
Photos: © Marino Ramazzotti

C. M. Interiors – Disseny i interiorisme S.C.P.
C/Madrazo 20-22 5º A, 08006 Barcelona, Spain
P +34 932 387 465
F +34 932 387 622
Mega Sport Showrooms
Photos: © Mauricio Salinas, Javier Pereda

Cadosh & Zimmermann
Malzstrasse 13, 8045 Zurich, Switzerland
P +41 444 618 989
F +41 444 618 990
cadosch@czarch.ch
www.czarch.ch
Stand for Eternit AG and Swisspor AG at Swissbau
Photos: © Fotoatelier Jürg Zimmermann

Chelsea Atelier Architect
245 7TH Avenue Suite 6A, New York, NY 10001, USA
P +1 212 255 3494
F +1 212 255 3495
info@chelseaatelier.com
ww.chelseaatelier.com
Reem Acra Showroom
Photos: © Björg Magnea

Christian Werner
Am Aarbach 14, 21279 Hollenstedt/Appel, Germany
P +49 416 521 2612
F +49 416 521 2613
office@christian-werner.com
www.christian-werner.com
Stand for Carpet Concept at Orgatec
Photos: © H. G. Esch
Stand for Rolf Benz at The International Furnishing Show (IMM)
Photos: © Karl Huber Fotodesign

CJ Studio
6F # 54, Lane 260 Kwang-fu, S. Rd, Taipei, Taiwan
P +886 227 738 366
F +886 227 738 365
cj@shi-chieh-lu.com
www.shi-chieh-lu.com
Showroom for Stephane Dou & Changlee Yugin
Photos: © Kuomin Lee

Claudio Carmona Parcerisa
C/Dr.Trias i Pujol 4, bajos 2ª, 08034 Barcelona, Spain
P +34 93 204 14 50
F +34 93 280 56 42
ccarmona@arquired.es
Rosa Clarà Showroom
Photos: © Eugeni Pons

D'Art Design Gruppe
Am Zollhafen 5, 41460 Neuss, Germany
P +49 213 140 307 0
F +49 213 140 307 89
pr@d-art-design.de
www.d-art-design.de
Stand for Alno AG at Eurocucina
Stand for Philips Lighting at Light & Building
Photos: © Jörg Hempel
Stand for D'Art Design Gruppe at Euroshop
Photos: © H. G. Esch, Andrea Borowski

Designrichtung/Jérôme Gessaga & Christof Hindermann
Luisenstrasse 25, 8005 Zurich, Switzerland
P +41 444 225 320
F +41 444 225 327
info@designrichtung.ch
www.designrichtung.ch
Denz AG Office Architecture Showroom
Geberit Vertriebs AG Showroom
Photos: © Tom Bisig

Dominic Niels Haag – Architektur Innenarchitektur Design
Rüdigerstrasse 11, 8045 Zurich, Switzerland
P +41 438 176 679
F +41 438 176 680
haag@haag-architektur.ch
www.haag-architektur.ch
Stand for SIA at Swissbau
Photos: © Reinhard Zimmermann

Dual Office
345 Vermont Street, San Francisco, CA 94103, USA
P +1 415 864 9900
www.dualoffice.com
Echo Handbag Showroom
Photos: © Björg Magnea

Esiete/Javier Pereda
C/Còrsega 290 1º 1ª, 08008 Barcelona, Spain
P +34 93 217 64 79
F +34 93 217 64 79
www.esiete.com
www.javierpereda.com
Mega Sport S.A. Showrooms
Photos: © Mauricio Salinas, Javier Pereda

Estudi Arola
C/Lope de Vega 106 3ª, 08005 Barcelona, Spain
P +34 93 307 53 69
F +34 93 307 46 70
info@estudiarola.com
www.estudiarola.com
Stand for Santa & Cole at Light & Building
Photos: © Nina Miralbell, Toni Lladó/Santa & Cole, Estudi Arola

Francesc Rifé
C/Escuelas Pías 25 bajos, 08017 Barcelona, Spain
P +34 93 414 12 88
F +34 93 241 28 14
f@rife-design.com
www.rife-design.com
Parkhouse Studio Showroom
Stand for Martínez Otero at International Furniture
Fair Valencia (FIM)
Photos: © Eugeni Pons
Stand for Bordonabe at Ofitec
Photos: © Francesc Rifé

Giorgio Borruso Design
333 Washington Blvd. 352, Marina del Rey, CA 90292, USA
P +1 310 821 9224
F +1 310 821 9350
info@borrusodesign.com
www.borrusodesign.com
Snaidero USA Showroom
Photos: © Benny Chan/Fotoworks

Ignasi Bonjoch
C/Bonavista 6 pral. 4ª, 08012 Barcelona, Spain
F +34 93 150 007
ignasi@bonjoch.com
www.bonjoch.com
Stand for Biosca & Botey at Construmat
Photos: © Eloi Bonjoch

Jaci Foti-Lowe
63 Exhibition Street, Melbourne, Victoria 3000, Australia
P +61 396 501 366
P +61 396 501 377
jlowe@hubfurniture.com.au
www.hubfurniture.com.au
Hub Furniture Living Lighting Showroom
Photos: © Trevor Mein

Joan Anguita & Rafael Berengena Arquitectes
C/Santa Perpètua 17 2-1, 08012 Barcelona, Spain
P +34 610 633 834
P +34 626 177 458
j.anguita@coac.net, maynegre@yahoo.es
Casa Delfín S.A. Showroom
Photos: Eugeni Pons

Joan Lao
C/Rosselló 214, 08008 Barcelona, Spain
P +34 93 415 75 36
F +34 93 415 51 53
exposicion@joanlao.com
www.joanlao.com
Joan Lao Showroom
Photos: © Eugeni Pons

Jump Studios
116 Commercial Street, Unit D103, E1 6NF London, UK
P +44 207 650 7800
F +44 207 650 7801
info@jump-studios.com
www.jump-studios.com
Stand for Levi's at Bread & Butter Barcelona
Photos: © Jump Studios

Jürgen Mayer H.
Bleibtreustrasse 54, 10623 Berlin, Germany
P +49 303 150 6117
F +49 303 150 6118
contact@jmayerh.de
www.jmayerh.de
Stand for NYA Nordiska at Design Annual
Photos: © Constantin Meyer, J. Mayer H.

KMS Team GmbH
Deroystraße 3-5, 80335 Munich, Germany
P +49 894 904 11 0
F +49 894 904 11 49
info@kms-team.de
www.kms-team.de
Stand for O2 at IFA
Photos: © Jens Weber

Knoll / Karen Stone
76 Ninth Avenue 11th Floor, New York, NY 10011, USA
Knoll Showroom
Photos: © Karen Stone, Marshal Safron Studios, Inc.

Kuhlmann Leavitt, Inc.
7810 Forsyth Blvd 2 W, St. Louis, MO 63105, USA
P + 1 314 725 6616
F + 1 314 725 6618
deanna@kuhlmannleavitt.com
www.kuhlmannleavitt.com
Stand for Formica Corporation at International
Home Builders' Show (IBS)
Photos: © Kuhlmann Leavitt, Inc.

Landini Associates
42 Davies Street, Surry Hills, NSW 2010, Australia
P +61 293 603 899
F +61 293 604 899
studio.aus@landiniassociates.com
www.landiniassociates.com
Harrolds Showroom
Photos: © Trevor Mein

LOC Arquitectos / Casillas & Sánchez Merchán
C/General Aranaz 25 L2, 28027 Madrid, Spain
P +34 91 371 74 24
F +34 91 371 72 03
locarquitectura@terra.es
Stand for ICEX at Exporta
Photos: © Eugeni Pons, Luis Casillas, María Jesús Sánchez

Paolo Cesaretti
Via Oxilia 23, 20127 Milan, Italy
P/F +39 226 809 419
contact@paolocesaretti.it
www.paolocesaretti.it
Hatria / Gruppo Marazzi Showroom
Photos: © Stefano Stagni / Serrap

Pavlik Design Team
1301 East Broward Blvd. 3rd Floor,
Ft. Lauderdale, FL 33301, USA
P +1 954 523 3300
F +1 954 523 2521
info@pavlikdesign.com
www.pavlikdesign.com
Neorest Showroom
Photos: © Pavlik Design Team

PS+A / Ludovica & Roberto Palomba
Via Zamenhof 17, 20136 Milan, Italy
P +39 289 401 695
F +39 258 118 350
web@palombaserafini.com
www.palombaserafini.com
Zucchetti Showroom (Barcelona)
Photos: © Espai d'Imatge Esdim

Richard Hywel Evans
36-37 Featherstone Street, EC1Y 8QZ London, UK
P +44 207 253 5358
F +44 207 253 5359
rhe@rhe.uk.com
www.rhe.uk.com
Modular Lighting UK Showroom
Photos: © Richard Hywel Evans

Ronan & Erwan Bouroullec
23 rue du Buisson Saint-Louis, 75010 Paris, France
P +33 142 004 033
F +33 142 005 211
info@bouroullec.com
www.bouroullec.com
Kvadrat Showroom
Photos: © Paul Tahon & Ronan Bouroullec

Saeta Estudi/Bet Cantallops, Pere Ortega
Passeig de Sant Joan 12 pral. 2ª, 08010 Barcelona, Spain
P/F +34 932 476 562
saeta@coac.net
www.saetaestudi.com
Stand for Layetana at Barcelona Meeting Point
Photos: © Xavier Berdala

Schindlerarchitekten
Forststrasse 62a, 70176 Stuttgart, Germany
P +49 711 656 779 77
F +49 711 656 779 79
schindlerarchitekten@t-online.de
www.schindlerarchitekten.de
Stand for Armstrong DLW AG at Domotex
Photos: © Werner Huthmacher

Schmidhuber & Partner, Schmidhuber & Kaindl
Architektur Innenarchitektur
Nederlinger Strasse 21, 80638 Munich, Germany
P +49 891 579 97 0
F +49 891 579 97 99
info@schmidhuber.de
www.schmidhuber.de
Samsung Brand Shop
Photos: © Yum Seung Hoon
Stand for O2 at CeBIT
Photos: © Jens Weber München

Studiomartino.5
Via Pasquale Stanislao Mancini 2, 00196 Rome, Italy
P +39 632 110 841
F +39 632 020 98
contact@studiomartino5.it
www.studiomartino5.it
Crovato Showroom
Photos: © Studio Ciapetti

Totems Communication & Architecture
Ludwigstrasse 59, 70176 Stuttgart, Germany
P +49 711 505 311 44
F +49 711 505 313 33
stuttgart@totems.com
www.totems.com
Stand for Bertrandt at International Motor Show (IAA)
Photos: © Totems Communication & Architecture
Stand for P&G Beauty at Milan Fashion Week
Photos: © Lulu Poletti Milano

© 2007 daab
cologne london new york

published and distributed worldwide by
daab gmbh
friesenstr. 50
d-50670 köln

p +49-221-913 927 0
f +49-221-913 927 20

mail@daab-online.com
www.daab-online.com

publisher ralf daab
rdaab@daab-online.com

creative director feyyaz
mail@feyyaz.com

editorial project by loft publications
© 2007 loft publications

editor research and text bridget vranckx

layout oriol serra juncosa
spanish translation verónica fajardo
french translation marion westerhoff
italian translation barbara burani
german translation sybille schellheimer

printed in spain
anman gràfiques del vallès, spain

isbn 978-3-937718-62-0